Egbert's Circus Games

Exercises for young violinists by
MARY COHEN

FABER _ff_ MUSIC

Contents

Tapping in the Tent Pegs	3	*finger tapping*
Hauling up the Ropes	4	*glissando*
Checking the Ropes	4	*left-hand pizzicato*
Stirring the Soup	5	*bow-hold*
Monkey climbing Flagpole	5	*bow-hold*
Pasting the Posters	6	*tone production*
'In Out'	7	*quick violin / bow placing*
Picking up Weights	8	*'golden tone', silent bowing*
Sea-Lion-Saw	9	*slurred string crossing / finger angles*
Egbert's Wobble	10	*bow placing / tone production*
Clever Acrobats	11	*arpeggios*
Clowns	12	*spiccato / lift and land*
Trapeze Artists	13	*slurred string crossing / finger angles*
Stately Waltz	14	*finger patterns 1 and 2*
March of the Parisian Poodles	15	*finger patterns 1 and 2 / martelé*
Grand Finale	16	
Grand Finale	17	*optional advanced duet part*
Teacher's Notes	18	

© 1991 by Faber Music Ltd
First published in 1991 by Faber Music Ltd
3 Queen Square London WC1N 3AU
Illustrations © 1991 by John Levers
Music drawn by Christopher Hinkins
Printed in England

Egbert's Circus Games

When Bim-Bam's Circus moves from town to town, there is always a lot of activity at the new site. Putting up the Big Top is a very important job.

Tapping in the Tent Pegs

(violin only, no bow needed)

a) *tap the tips of the fingers on the right-hand shoulder of the violin*
b) *tap the notes in the correct place on the fingerboard (NB not pizzicato)*

Hauling up the Ropes

*Play glissandos with harmonic pressure only (using the
third or fourth fingers) up and down the fingerboard on
all four strings in turn. Start on the G string so that the
ropes get higher and higher. Adjust the elbow to reach the
lower strings comfortably and use long slow bows.*

When the Big Top is in place, Egbert checks that
all the ropes are secure.

Checking the Ropes

(left-hand pizzicato throughout)

Stirring the Soup

(bow only)

Make a bow hold with firm but flexible fingers, pointing the bow up to the ceiling. Pretend that you are stirring thick soup with the heel of your bow. From time to time 'shake' salt, pepper and other ingredients into the pot from the heel of your bow. Keep ckecking that you have a good bow hold.

While he is eating his soup, Egbert watches Mirabelle the monkey putting up the circus flag.

Monkey climbing Flagpole

Make your right-hand fingers crawl up and down the stick so that the bow remains as still as possible while your arm gets higher and higher. It's tricky coming down!

Mr. Bim-Bam pastes posters advertising his circus all around the town.

Pasting the Posters

Next morning, Mr. Bim-Bam organises Keep Fit exercises before breakfast.

'In Out'

(make sure you have plenty of room on each side before you start)

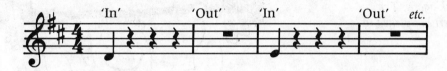

Picking up Weights

Play long, very slow bows silently on the top of the bridge. Count the seconds to see how long you can make the bow last from the heel to the point and back again. The number tells you the weight that Egbert has picked up today.

After breakfast, rehearsals begin in earnest. The two sea-lions
balance big yellow balls on their noses and rock up and down on
a see-saw.

Sea-Lion-Saw

When they've finished, Egbert tries to stand up in the middle of the see-saw but he wobbles rather a lot!

Egbert's Wobble

(play in middle of bow)

(carry on up the A major scale; then transpose into other keys)

Egbert watches the acrobats jumping on each other's shoulders
to form a human pyramid!

Acrobats

'carefully rehearsing'

Clever Acrobats

(alternative ending, use harmonic)

Egbert joins the clowns as they rush around the ring bouncing big coloured balls.

Clowns

One of the balls has lost its bounce.

Variation *(lift and land without any bounce)*

etc.

Some of the acrobats perform a clever act on the flying trapeze.

Trapeze Artists

14 Ernest the elephant dances with Polly the parrot.

Stately Waltz

They are followed by a troupe of poodles, who prance around
the ring on their hind legs.

March of the Parisian Poodles

(poodles balancing!)

(poodles balancing!)

Everyone joins in the rehearsal for the

Grand Finale

Grand Finale

(optional advanced duet part)

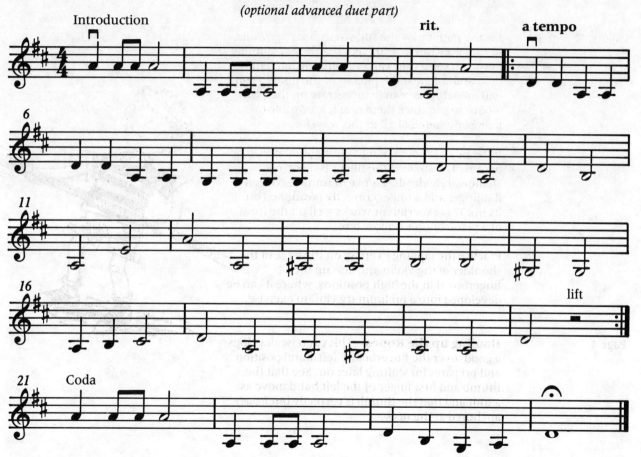

Page 3

Let the pupils play the tune as ordinary *pizzicato*, so that they can hear the pitches they are aiming for. Then see if they can tap with the left hand only and still hear the pitches of the notes. (You will probably have to demonstrate on their own violins to convince them that it is possible to make any sound at all in this way!)

If the pupil is not making a clear sound it may be because the angle of the finger is incorrect. Demonstrate the difference in sound between a flat finger and a finger correctly positioned on its tip. This experiment works well on the front of a piano or on a hollow box.

Practise the tapping exercise on the edge of the shoulder of the violin and also up the fingerboard in the high positions, where it can be developed into a preliminary vibrato exercise.

Page 4

Hauling up the Ropes – This exercise develops a good 'over the fingerboard' left-hand position and prepares for shifting later on. See that the thumb and first finger of the left hand move as a unit and that the thumb is correctly but *loosely* anchored at the neck.

Checking the Ropes – This exercise develops finger strength and facility in the left hand. Transpose into D major and G major, ensuring that the elbow adjusts under the violin while the pupil plays on the lower strings, so that the hand is correctly balanced and not straining. As a separate exercise, practise positioning the fingers silently on all four strings in turn. Start on the E string, and as the fingers move leftwards to reach the lower strings, encourage a natural elbow movement in the opposite direction.

Page 5

Discuss 'a good bow hold', and show the three points of balance and contact (first finger, little finger and edge of thumb).

Monkey Climbing is an old favourite! The left-hand fingers have to crawl up and down the stick so that the bow remains virtually still while the arm gets higher and higher. Coming back down is the really tricky bit!

Page 6

The idea of 'brushing' the paste is to develop a good flowing legato stroke with smooth bow changes. At first use the middle/upper half of the bow, but later come back and try to encourage use of the lower half. Many pupils are very reluctant to use the six inches of hair nearest to the heel, usually because they are not positioning their thumb and fingers correctly as they change direction. Check that the thumb is making contact with the stick at an oblique angle on the edge of the nail and not too far over on the tip. (If the thumb and middle two fingers of the right hand form a circle without the bow in the hand, the second finger touches the thumb at roughly the same place at which the thumb should touch the stick of the bow.)

Transpose into D major and G major also, to ensure good arm and elbow levels on all strings.

20   Page 7

Begin with the violin held normally in first position and play the first note with a ringing tone. Next, move the left hand up to the shoulder of the violin and with a firm hold, take the instrument away from the chin and hold it out to the side as far as possible. At the same time stretch out the bow-arm in the opposite direction, while keeping a good bow hold. Resume normal violin and bow position and continue in the same way up the scale.

Page 8

The 'Golden Tone' exercise. This develops control and also improves tone production if practised regularly. It is a good one to do while the left hand is having a rest! Aim to take at least 60–90 seconds to get from one end of the bow to the other.

Page 9

The playing fingers must be angled so they can remain held down without 'catching' the open string. Transpose into A major and make a longer piece by playing D major – A major – D major.

Page 10

An exercise aimed at achieving good hair/string contact and finding the correct amount of bow weight necessary for good tone production, which can also be adapted to practise the *martelé* stroke.

Place the middle of the bow on the string with flat hair, then quickly drop and raise the hand over and over again so that the bow 'see-saws' silently on the spot. If the movement is done correctly with a relaxed arm, the elbow will move as a counterbalance in the opposite direction. This movement also looks like a see-saw.

Page 11

Play also in the keys of G major and A major and try with different rhythmic variations. After the second finger pattern is established, use the two-octave G major arpeggio.

First, practise a preliminary exercise for *spiccato*:
allow each pupil to find the best bouncing point
for their own bow by using a vertical movement
only. (This should be somewhere in the middle,
otherwise check the bow carefully!) The best
bounce is achieved with flat hair and plenty
of relaxed arm movement: only at the heel is
spiccato best controlled by wrist/finger action.
Then add a little 'swingboat' action to get a true
spiccato stroke.

The variation needs a very relaxed and flexible
bow-hold if the bow is to land without bouncing.
If the bounce is difficult to eliminate, try getting
the pupil to remove each finger of the right hand
in turn and gently tap the stick with it a few
times before resuming a more relaxed hold.
(The wood of the bow should be held securely,
either by the teacher or by the pupil's left hand.)
It sometimes helps pupils to think of their
fingers as sponges, soaking up the vibrations
which result when they 'land'.

Angle the fingers so that they can remain held
down where marked without catching on the
open string. If this is difficult, adjusting the
elbow under the violin and checking the
thumb position may help to achieve a better
hand balance.

Many children become confused at first when they have to cope with two-finger patterns. It sometimes helps them to remember where the notes are if they think of the notes as laid out in a grid (like a game of hopscotch!) Encourage them to draw and fill in their own 'grids' as part of their weekly practising until they can find and play any random note. B♮ and B♭ are particularly difficult to remember, so try transposing **Stately Waltz** into G major and discussing the resultant notes.

SCROLL

G	D	A	E
A	E	B	F♯
B♭	F	C	G
B	F♯	C♯	G♯
C	G	D	A

FINGERBOARD

↓

BRIDGE

When a new piece has both left-hand and right-hand problems, it is often useful to learn the notes in the ordinary *détaché* style and then practise the difficult bow-stroke first on one note, and eventually in a familiar scale. *Martelé* can be explained as a short, sharp 'pinch' to spark the bow into movement (like striking a match). It also helps to think of an upward thumb pressure being resisted by the fingers.

G	D	A	E